Personal Verses

Poetic Lessons From Biblical Personalities

George A Bowers, Sr.

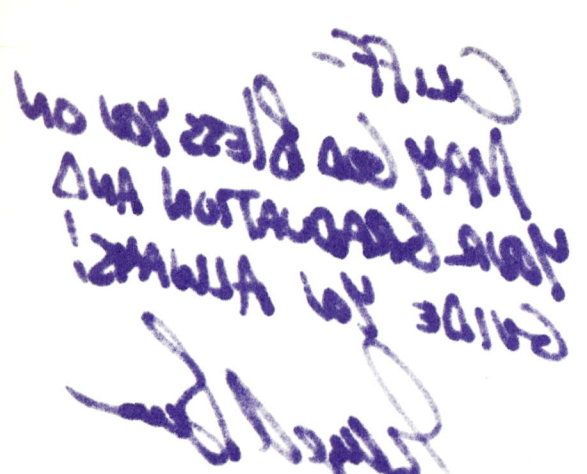

Cliff –
May God Bless you on your graduation and guide you always!

George B.

Copyright © 2014 by George A Bowers, Sr.,
All Rights reserved.

Personal Verses
By George A Bowers, Sr.

ISBN # 978-1-304-85751-4

Cover Photo by the Author

DEDICATION

This book of poems is written for the Glory of God and the praise of His Son, Jesus Christ and is dedicated to two great personalities in my life, my son Allen and my daughter Mary. They are each very different, but each very special and have taught me much more about life than I've ever taught them.

Special thanks to my dear wife, Nancy for her encouragement and prayers.

Contents

Preface   6

Old Testament Personalities   7

   Gideon and Midian   8
   A Weak Strong Man   10
   Boaz's Story   13
   A Lesson From David   15
   Ecclesiastes   17
   David and His Son   19
   Solomon's Rhyme   21
   Tragic Trainwreck   23
   Noah   25
   Jacob   26
   Achin' Achan   27
   Sampson   28
   Naomi   29
   Ruth   29
   Solomon   30
   Jehu   30
   Jeremiah   31
   Esther   31

New Testament Personalities   **33**

Mary's Brother   **34**
Faithful Philip   **38**
Judas   **41**
The Money Plan Man   **43**
Saul   **47**
Peter   **47**
Christ's Work   **48**

Preface

Many of the characters that we read about on the pages of the Bible can teach us much about ourselves. They struggled with the same issues, shared some of the same passions, and enjoyed some of the same blessings as us.

If we would know more about ourselves, about God and about our relationship with Him, we would do well to look to these men and women on the pages of Scripture.

OLD TESTAMENT PERSONALITIES

THESE THINGS HAPPENED TO THEM as examples and were written down as warnings for us, on whom the fulfillment of the ages has come. So, if you think you are standing firm, be careful that you don't fall! No temptation has seized you except what is common to man. And God is faithful; he will not let you be tempted beyond what you can bear. But when you are tempted, he will also provide a way out so that you can stand up under it.

1 Corinthians 10:11-13

A wise person once told me that no man lives long enough to make all the mistakes himself, so we must learn from the mistakes of others. In the verses above, Paul reminds us that all that happened to God's people throughout the Old Testament should serve as examples for us to learn from. Let us see what lessons their lives teach us.

GIDEON AND MIDIAN

November 2012

THE HEBREWS WERE OPPRESSED, by the people of Midian,
So God raised up a judge, by the name of Gideon.
God chose this trembling coward, to use and greatly bless,
And called him from his threshing, down in his old winepress.
"You are the one I've picked, to drive out all those foes,
And deliver all my people, from all these stressful woes.
But first you must destroy, the idols in this place,
For they are what's brought on, all this deep disgrace."
So Gideon cut them down, and then he burned them too,
God's people must be holy, they must be pure and true.
But Gideon wasn't sure, and placed a fleece before the Lord,
The ground was desert dry, but from the fleece he poured.

And then he did embark, upon his sacred quest,
He chose thirty-two thousand men, the strongest and the best.
But God said that's too many, I've got a different plan,
Take them to the water's edge, and there I'll choose each man.
The ones who lap like dogs, will be included in this story,
They are the small minority, who will achieve My glory.
And when the count was made, three hundred's what remained,
Not so very many, but what God had ordained.
So Gideon took them up, with a sword and pot and lamp,
They spread out on the hills, around the enemy camp.
"For Gideon and for God!" The Israelites did shout!
And all their enemies, began to grope about.
And when the trumpet blew, they broke their old clay pots,
And brought fear to the Midianites, lying on their cots.
They rose up from their slumber, confused and drunken too,
And began to kill each other, like men without a clue.
And before that night was over, the victory was the Lord's,
The Israelites had won, and barely used their swords.
The people were delivered, the men had quite a story,
But this victory was the Lord's, and He got all the glory.
So when you are afraid, and you don't know what to do,
Give it all to God, and let Him fight for you!

A Weak Strong Man

April 2013

SAMSON HIMSELF WAS A MIGHTY STRONG MAN,
The strongest, in fact, in the whole entire land
The hair upon his head, was very, very long
And the biceps of his arms, were very, very strong.
He killed a thousand men with a donkey's raw jawbone,
And with his own bare hands killed a lion like a stone.
One night they trapped him tightly, down in Gaza's halls
But he ripped their city gates clean off their stony walls.
He carried them atop of yonder rising hill,
With nothing but his might and strong resolute will.

His muscles didn't come from hours in at the gym,
For the Lord had especially gifted and strongly strengthened him.
As a Nazarite from birth, he drank no bubbly wine
Nor any other product that came from off the vine.
And never was his hair to be cut from off his head,
Nor the paths of sin were his feet to ever tread.
To deliver God's people was his holy call,
From Philistine intruders and their enemies all.
To lead and judge his people, he did it all so well,
He did all these things until he sadly fell.
For though his super strength was surely very great,
He had one major weakness of a character trait.
He couldn't stay away from the pretty merry maids
Who all seemed so entranced, to love his long black braids.
And one of those young ladies, Delilah was her name,
Seduced old mighty Samson by playing an old game.
As he laid upon her lap, she cried to him that night,
So he told her the whole secret, of his strength and might.
And then she went to work as he drifted off to sleep.
She cut his lengthy locks for some silver coins, so cheap.

And when he woke back up at the breaking of the dawn,
He discovered very quickly that his strength was wholly gone.
His captors rudely gouged, and took out his once proud eyes,
Shackled him all up and paraded out their prize.
But as the time went by, His mighty strength returned,
And for his own revenge, his bitter heart sore yearned.
And one day at a party as they all danced around,
Samson with his might brought the whole house down.
He killed more of his enemies, upon his dying day
Than he had in all his life and all along his way.
But it didn't have to end in this tragic fashion,
If Samson had controlled his raging lustful passion.
Men, learn this lesson, from Samson big and strong,
Lust will bind you tightly and steer you totally wrong.
Don't end up so weak, getting bound and cruelly blind,
Let the Holy Spirit control, both your body and mind.

Boaz's Story

May 2011

My Name Is Mr. Boaz,

    I've come from threshing wheat,
And now I want to sit right down
    and have some bread to eat!
But who is this dear lady,
    as pretty as can be?
I think I'll take a little time,
    to find what I can see.
From all my careful research,
    what I do believe is truth,
This maiden in my field today,
    is known as fine Miss Ruth.

Her husband passed away,
> down in her own homeland,

And now she's moved up here,
> with his mother and his clan.

She's given up her idols,
> to serve the one true God.

Among the women nowadays,
> that is pretty odd.

I think I'll ask her out,
> she seems a perfect gift,

And I'll bet her sorry spirits,
> could use a little lift.

So that is how it started out,
> her gathering wheat for bread,

And now we're married very nice,
> with a little son, Obed!

A Lesson From David

April 2013

Life For David Had Become Quite Good,
>As a gift from God, he understood.

Conquering enemies on every side,
>His gold and silver had been multiplied.

Reigning in the palace as the Israeli king,
>He really didn't want for anything.

Until that evening on his palace roofline,
>When he looked down and saw Bathsheba so fine.

Bathing her body so that she could be clean,
>But not in a spot where she couldn't be seen.

David sent for her, in royal fashion,

He refused to subdue his rising passion.
And there in the palace he committed great sin,
    And then sent the woman back home again.

But she was now pregnant and would bear his son,
    So David tried to cover the adultery he'd done.
His plan didn't work, while he tried not to hurt her,
    But he finally resorted to cold blooded murder.
That cleared the way for the two to be married,
    And justify his child that she now carried.

But this was not hidden from the eyes of the Lord,
    And David's house would pay with a lasting sword.
This passing pleasure would cause much pain,
    And on David's clean record, make an ugly stain.
Although he was forgiven, David's heart would break,
    And for years to come, keep his nights awake.

Oh learn a lesson from David's life,
    Keep your love at home with your own sweet wife.

Ecclesiastes
April 2013

S͏olomon S͏earched F͏or S͏anity
But all he found was vanity.
Although he had great earthly fame.
"Life has no meaning!" he did proclaim
For he made his search upon his own,
Without his God, yes, all alone.

He sought for it in worldly pleasure
And also in rich golden treasure.
He searched for it in drink and food,
And in his women which he wooed.

But in spite of all he'd had and done,
He found no meaning beneath the sun.
No matter how hard he seemed to try,
"It's all for naught!" was his vain cry.

One thing he found that still is true,
All over this earth, there's nothing new,
From the time we're born until we die,
He said it's useless to question why.
Without the Lord, life's empty, vain,
Filled with struggle, hardship, and pain.

But it all makes sense when God is there,
Even though our lives will be unfair.
There's hope and meaning beyond the grave,
And that which Jesus to us gave.
So look beyond the struggles of earth,
To heaven's eternal surpassing worth!

DAVID AND HIS SON
April 2013

DAVID WOULD BECOME THE SHEPHERD KING
Who would write grand Psalms for all to sing,
He killed a lion and a big black bear,
As he kept his sheep with loving care.
When he went to visit his brothers three,
The ones who served in Saul's army,
He was quite surprised by everyone's fears,
Of the giant, Goliath and his taunting jeers.
Day by day he threatened with boasts,
While no one thought of the Lord of Hosts.
Till David showed up with his sling and five stones,
And brought down all of his proud giant bones.
Anointed by Samuel and chosen to lead,
His place in the kingdom was guaranteed.
But he had to wait years till the time was right,
Depended on God instead of using his might.
Chased by Saul through deserts and caves,
David all the while, trusted God who saves.
Spared the life of his enemy twice,

Bided his time paying patience's price.
And then one day when the time was right,
He became the king with hardly a fight.
He enlarged the borders and secured the land,
Ruling over Israel with a strong, but fair hand.
Brave and fearless, intelligent and smart,
Honest and true and after God's own heart.
Blessed by God with a well-known name,
Chosen by Him for worldwide fame.
A kingdom to endure both now and ever,
An eternal dynasty none could fully sever.

His seed would rule forevermore,
What a great grand promise God had in store.
For the Son of David would later arrive,
To prove God's promise was still alive.
And one day yet, He'll come again,
To establish His reign that shall never end.
Peace and justice throughout all the land.
The entire universe under His command,
Even so, Come Jesus, we can only pray,
For the Son of David's return one day.

SOLOMON'S RHYME

April 2013

DAVID HAD TAUGHT HIM TO PRAY AND SING,
And Solomon his son, was now the king.
Reigning well over Israel's land,
Would require a skillful and wise man.
And although he had an instructed tongue,
Solomon himself was pretty young.
At Gibeon's altar he gave to the Lord,
And lavishly worshipped and freely adored.
And that very night while sleeping good,
God came into his neighborhood.
Due to his generous altar fire,
God offered him his heart's desire.
What would he choose, great earthly wealth?

Or a long full life with perfect health?
Success out on the battlefield?
Strength to whom all others yield?
Leisure and pleasure and worldly fun?
Solomon chose from these, not one.
Instead that thing for which he yearned,
Was a heart with wisdom to discern.
To know the truth with keen insight,
And to know the difference between wrong and right.
And because this was his wise request,
God gave him this and all the rest.
He became the richest, wisest king,
With knowledge of most everything.
People came to him from far and near,
His wise insight to gladly hear.
He built the kingdom, ruled her well,
For many years before he fell.
His many wives led him astray
And caused his heart to disobey.
Although he was so very wise,
He couldn't control his lustful eyes.
So use your wisdom and understand
And learn this lesson from the wisest man.

Tragic Trainwreck

May 2013

Solomon had everything he'd ever need,
To serve as the king, rule well and succeed.
Honor and armies, much silver and gold,
Respect of the people, both young and old.
Counselors many, and wisdom as well,
A king with more strength than any could tell.
But he strayed away far from what he needed most,
His wives turned his heart from the great Lord of Hosts!
Worshipping idols and bringing them in,
He lost his whole nation directly to sin.

God said that ten tribes would from him be torn,
But one would remain as to David He'd sworn.
And sure enough later, just after he died,
Rebellion in Israel was soon multiplied.
His son took the throne by the name Rehoboam,
But he was opposed by one Jeroboam.
The Kingdom of David with riches and wonder
Was now torn in two and riven asunder.
And even as Israel was split into halves,
The King of the North set up golden calves.
The people, they sinned and strayed from their Lord,
The One who had saved them, they should have adored.
Such a sad ending to such a good start,
Let's each learn a lesson and guard close our heart,
To stray from our Savior, we cannot afford,
Let's worship and honor and obey the Lord.

NOAH

*Noah was a righteous man, blameless among the
people of his time, and he walked with God.*
Genesis 6:9-10

GOD SENT A STRONG MESSAGE TO NOAH
To save people and pigs and protozoa
He built a big boat,
Put on his raincoat,
And spent forty wet nights with a boa!

JACOB

*So Jacob was left alone, and a man
wrestled with him till daybreak.
Genesis 32:24*

JACOB WAS QUITE A DECEIVER
And liked to be quite the receiver,
But God showed him the light,
As they wrestled one night,
And then Jacob became a believer!

Achin' Achan

Achan replied, "It is true! I have sinned against the Lord, the God of Israel. This is what I have done: When I saw in the plunder a beautiful robe from Babylonia, two hundred shekels of silver and a wedge of gold weighing fifty shekels, I coveted them and took them. They are hidden in the ground inside my tent, with the silver underneath."
Joshua 7:20-21

There Once was a Man Named Achan
Who thought he'd get by with sin fakin'
While doing his duty,
He stole him some booty
And for-ever after was achin'!

SAMPSON

While they were in high spirits, they shouted, "Bring out Samson to entertain us." So they called Samson out of the prison, and he performed for them.
Judges 16:25

SAMPSON WAS A MAN THAT WAS RARE,
He had him the longest of hair,
His muscles were strong,
But his passions were wrong,
He was put into jail and died there.

Naomi

There Once Was A Woman, Naomi,
Who had to leave her old homey,
She went down to the south,
And got food for her mouth,
Where the soil was better and loamy!

So Naomi returned from Moab accompanied by Ruth the Moabitess, her daughter-in-law, arriving in Bethlehem as the barley harvest was beginning.
Ruth 1:22

Ruth

There Once Was A Woman Named Ruth
Whose husband died in his youth,
She stayed with his mother,
And found her another,
And became a grandparent of Truth!

SOLOMON

*As Solomon grew old, his wives turned his heart
after other gods, and his heart was not fully devoted to
the Lord his God, as the heart of David his father had been.
1 Kings 11:4*

DAVID'S SON WAS THE WISEST OF MEN,
But his brains didn't keep him from sin,
His wives turned his heart
From the God of his start
All that's left now is, "what might have been."

JEHU

*The driving is like that of Jehu son of Nimshi —
he drives like a madman." 2 Kings 9:20*

THERE ONCE WAS A MAN NAMED JEHU
Who drove pretty much just like we do
All in a rush
To avoid all the crush,
I'd hate to see him on a ski-doo!

JEREMIAH

*So they took Jeremiah and put him into the
cistern of Malkijah, the king's son, which was in
the courtyard of the guard. They lowered Jeremiah
by ropes into the cistern; it had no water in it, only
mud, and Jeremiah sank down into the mud.
Jeremiah 38:6*

A MAN NAMED JEREMIAH ONCE CRIED,
Because the faith of his people had died,
The truth he did tell
He ended up in a well,
But you can't say that he never tried!

ESTHER

*Who knows but that you have come to royal position
for such a time as this?"
Esther 4:14*

THERE ONCE WAS A WOMAN NAMED
ESTHER,
Who had a big trial come to test her,
She did the right thing
And spoke to the king,
And Haman was hanged as a jester.

NEW TESTAMENT PERSONALITIES

For everything that was written
in the past was written to teach us,
so that through endurance and
the encouragement of the
Scriptures we might have hope.

Romans 15:4

*We often view Biblical characters as
very different from ourselves when in
reality they were very much like us.
The Disciples that walked with Jesus
and the other individuals who lived in that
same era can still teach us much about
our own lives. Let's see what we can learn.*

Mary's Brother
April 2012

Lazarus Was A Fine Good Man,
    upright in every way,
And in a joyful mood to boot,
    almost on every day.
It was a little odd then,
    to see him feeling down,
We sisters noticed right away,
    when we returned from town.
We gave him chicken soup,
    and sent him up to bed.
He seemed to have a fever
    according to his head.

And as the next day came,
> he seemed a good bit worse,

This illness that he had,
> was more than we could nurse.

We all were quite concerned
> and we had a sinking feeling,

We called our good friend Jesus,
> for we had seen Him healing.

But as we waited for Him,
> Lazarus up and died,

Both Martha and I
> were deeply grieved and cried.

We buried him right soon,
> as custom told us to,

While friends and neighbors both came by
> with cards and tasty stew.

And finally on the fourth day,
> after his dying date,

Who shows up but Jesus,
> how could He be so late?

Each of us sad sisters,
> told Him as we cried,

"Lord if You had been here,
> our brother would not have died."

Jesus wept there with us
> our grief moved Him to tears,

Then He tried to build our faith
> and banish all our fears.

"I am the Resurrection,
> and I am the Life!

Trusting in My holy power,
> will save you from death's strife."

And then with loudest voice,
> yelling through the gloom,

"Lazarus come forth!"
> He shouted to the tomb.

And while all of us were watching,
> Lazarus came out!

Jesus said, "Take off His wraps,
> so he can move about."

We were all astounded;
> we couldn't believe our eyes,

We'd never seen a dead man,
> after four long days, arise.

Some were passing out,
> but I could only stare,

We could do nothing else,
> but bow down and worship there.

We all became aware that day,
> that Jesus, He was God,

For no one but He has the power,
> to bring back from the sod.

I now do not fear death,
> that nasty ugly thing,

For Jesus conquered it for us,
> and has removed its sting.

We all will face death's door
> and go down to the grave,

So be sure you know this One,
> with power to raise and save.

FAITHFUL PHILIP

April 2012

GOD SENT DEACON PHILIP
to a desert road location
To meet a leading man
from the Ethiopian nation.
Of this very reason,
Philip had no single hint,
But because the Spirit led him,
he got right up and went.
And as he stood by yonder road,
perhaps praying there and such.
A royal chariot came along
with a queen's own fancy touch.
Within it was her eunuch
that managed all her gold,

And all the rest of her great wealth
and all she bought and sold.
He was reading from the Bible
but he didn't understand,
So Philip climbed right up
to give the man a hand.
He told him all of Jesus,
of His death and resurrection,
And how He'd died to save us
from our sin and insurrection.
He told him how this news
was intended for all men,
Regardless of their status
or the color of their skin.
That we're all of Adam's line
in a single human race.
Then the man believed in Jesus,
right there in that desert place.
He stopped his chariot short
by a little desert pool,
And had his brother baptize him
in water clear and cool.

Then the Spirit carried Phil
to another destination
While the man went on his way
with new hope and great salvation.
We understand that new convert
spread the Word to many others,
And expanded Jesus' Kingdom
to his sisters and his brothers.
I'm thankful faithful Philip
obeyed the Lord that day
And pointed this poor seeking man
to Jesus' only way.
And I hope we'll too be faithful
and that God is glorified,
As we point each lost and wandering soul
to Jesus' precious side.

JUDAS

April 2012

HE'D NEVER BRAG NOR PROUDLY BOAST,

    The one we trusted in the most.

    We even let him keep our cash,

    Trustworthy, honest, never rash.

We'd gone with him on mission trips,

    We never doubted his friendship.

We prayed together, bared our souls,

    And shared each other's old bed rolls.

    We drove out demons side by side,

    Cried together when Lazarus died.

He could preach well, and loud, and strong,

    Teach and heal and lead a song.

So we couldn't believe when he betrayed,

    For the thirty pieces he was paid.

How could he sell his Loved One so?

I guess we'll never fully know.

For filthy lucre and silver's shine,

He sold the Messiah, God's Son Divine.

Knowing this he shared that meal,

I wonder how the Lord did feel?

But I can tell you we were shocked,

That night our world was wholly rocked.

By one on whom we could depend

One of our own, our trusted friend.

And then he went and took his life,

Believing that would end his strife.

What a sad and tragic bitter end

We all wondered, "What might have been?"

But we must forgive and let him go,

Even though it's hard and healing's slow.

This is the way that Jesus led,

And we must follow with heart and head.

And let's be sure not to do the same,

May we never betray our Lord's dear name.

Being true to him to the very end

Our Savior, Lord, Redeemer, Friend.

THE MONEY PLAN MAN
Judas's Story

April 2011

I FOLLOWED HIM FOR THREE LONG YEARS,

And shed for Him both sweat and tears.

I tried to obey His every word

My hungry soul His teaching stirred!

I watched Him heal the blind and lame,

Then with His power I did the same!

It was so amazing, something new,

Finally something I could do!

We'd soon push out those Roman jerks,

With force and strength and deadly works!

This Man would lead us, forge the way,

We twelve would follow and obey.

I was the one to keep our stash,

The coins and precious little cash.
We never seemed to have enough,
We lived like paupers, very rough.
He tried to give it all away,
No business head at all, I'd say.
So now and then I'd slip a mite,
To cover my trouble, 'twas only right.
And then the waste on yesterday,
Perfume worth one year's full time pay,
Poured out like water on His feet,
For Jesus to go 'round smelling sweet.
That was it, the final straw,
I made my way to the High Priest's hall.
I'll push this Christ to make His stand,
Simply shove a bit to force His hand.
And in the process, build our bank,
Thirty silver pieces with me to thank.
He'll set this country back to right,
I'll start His arrest this very night.
He'll have to show His mighty power,
Did He not just say this was His hour?
When the time is right I'll plant a kiss,
They'll know which One and never miss.

But wait, He's showing no resistance,
He's going along with their insistence.
How can this be? Tomorrow He'll die!
For I heard the priests cry, "Crucify!"
What did I do? My plans backfired!
This surely is not what I desired.
I've betrayed my Lord who loved me so,
I'll return the money, they'll let Him go.
But now they say that they will not,
What can I do? My foolish plot!!
I'll throw the coins down at their feet,
And my part then will be complete.
But still I can't escape this guilt!
This foolish scheme that I have built!
I should've listened to Him last night,
I should know by now He's always right!
I've done these evil deeds in vain,
I'll take my life and end my pain...

And so for Judas, a bitter fate,
And an even worse eternal state.
For even this, Christ could forgive,
And a new clean life, Judas could live.

But he shut the door, refused God's grace,

And turned away from His loving face.

O may we then learn this today,

Let us not scheme, but just obey.

Following Jesus with trust complete,

Until in Heaven, our Lord, we meet.

SAUL

*About noon as I came near Damascus,
suddenly a bright light from heaven
flashed around me.*
Acts 22:6

THERE ONCE WAS A MAN NAMED SAUL,
Who later changed it to Paul.
He saw a bright light,
And that changed his whole fight,
From killing to spreading "The Call."

PETER

*"Then, Lord," Simon Peter replied,
"not just my feet but my hands
and my head as well!"*
John 13:9

A MAN NAMED PETER EXISTED,
He, the Lord's feet-washing resisted.
He soon said, "OK,"
"Push me in all the way!"
And many more souls he enlisted.

CHRIST'S WORK

JESUS IS LORD OF THE EARTH,
He died to give me new birth,
He saved me from sin,
His joy entered in,
And gave my life infinite worth.

      I hope you have enjoyed your time with Personal Verses as much as I have enjoyed sharing these poems with you. Even more, I hope that you know the One who inspired these words, Jesus Christ. He is the Son of God who came to wash away our sins by His blood which was shed on the cross.

      If you don't know Him, take a minute now to pray. Tell God that you love Him and that you believe Jesus Christ is His Son and ask Him to forgive your sins. Turn from any sin in your life and with the help of His Holy Spirit, begin to live each day for Jesus.

      If you just prayed that prayer or if you already know Jesus as your Savior, be sure to be actively involved in His Body, the Church and use whatever gifts God has given you to serve Him. It is my hope that if we've never met on this earth, that I'll get to meet you some day in Heaven! Until then, may God richly bless you as you serve Him.

                                          Blessings, George

Other Books By
George A. Bowers, Sr.

Valley Verses

A collection of over 40 poems on Birds, Fish, Hunting, the Shenandoah River, Lover's Lane, Gospel Lessons, Caverns, Jesus' Cross, Holidays and more!

Valley Verses Volume II

A collection of 46 poems on Creation, Lessons from Nature, Old and New Testament characters, Christmas, Hunting Laughter and many more Just for Fun!

Blessings

This is a collection of modern day parables from everyday life that can be read devotionally or shared with others. Through the pages of this book, you will learn to know yourself and God better.

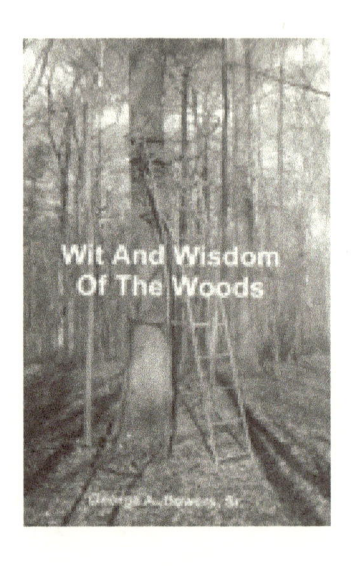

Wit and Wisdom Of The Woods

A collection of over 70 outdoor poems especially for the outdoorsman and hunter. Hunting Tales, Turkey Poems, Talking Animals, Creative Genius, A Salute to Trees and much more!

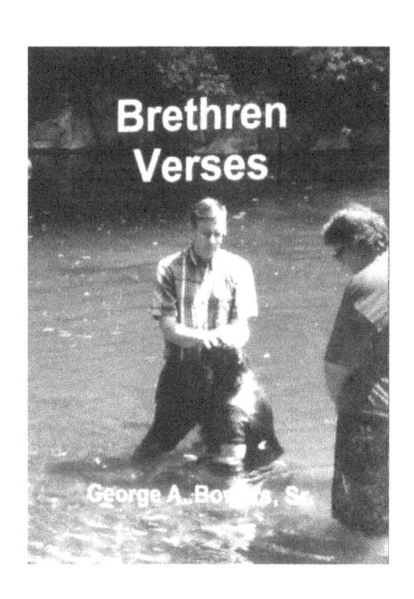

Brethren Verses

These poems celebrate the history and doctrine of the Church of the Brethren. There are poems on Feetwashing, Love Feast, Baptism, the Prayer Veil, Annual Conference, and many, many more.

Holy Verses

Whether planning a Good Friday service, Easter Sunrise, or just seeking personal devotion, these poems keep the focus on Jesus. From Palm Sunday to Calvary and from Gethsemane to the Tomb, these poems are sure to enrich your Holy Week.